PRAYERS & PROMISES
FOR
Parents

BroadStreet
P U B L I S H I N G

CONTENTS

Introduction

From the moment they are born, our children hold a prominent place in our hearts. We begin to worry about their wellbeing even before they draw their first breath. It can become overwhelming if we let it. What can we do? Pray and claim God's promises over their lives!

Prayers & Promises for Parents is a topically organized collection that guides you through themes of protection, peace, joy, purpose, rest, and more. Encouraging Scriptures, heartfelt prayers, and prompting questions give you an opportunity to think more deeply about the joy and truth found in God's Word.

Find encouragement and peace by staying connected to God and believing in his promises. Ask him for wisdom to help you guide, comfort, and nurture the children he has blessed you with. He is with you, he is for you, and he hears you when you pray!

Acceptance

"The Father gives me the people who are mine.
Every one of them will come to me,
and I will always accept them."

JOHN 6:37 NCV

"The LORD does not see as man sees; for man looks at the
outward appearance, but the LORD looks at the heart."

1 SAMUEL 16:7 NKJV

If God is for us, who can be against us?

ROMANS 8:31 ESV

In love he chose us before he laid the foundation of
the universe! Because of his great love, he ordained
us, so that we would be seen as holy in his eyes with an
unstained innocence.

EPHESIANS 1:4 TPT

God who includes all, thank you for not rejecting us. You have gone to great lengths to include each and every one of us in your family. You didn't just elect us as servants, and you didn't stop at making us friends; you called us into the closest relationship with you. You have promised to not reject any who call on your name. If my children are hurt from being rejected, whatever the reason was, I pray for restoration and healing for them. Please, communicate your love for them, and give them confidence in the fact that you will never abandon them.

How does God's acceptance of you help you be more accepting of others?

Anger

Don't get angry.
Don't be upset; it only leads to trouble.
Evil people will be sent away,
but those who trust the Lord will inherit the land.

Psalm 37:8-9 ncv

Everyone should be quick to listen, slow to speak and
slow to become angry, because human anger does not
produce the righteousness that God desires.

James 1:19-20 niv

"Don't sin by letting anger control you."
Don't let the sun go down while you are still angry.

Ephesians 4:26 nlt

Father, how we view you changes our whole worldview. We are transformed by who we think you are and what we know of your interactions with humanity. Our kids are like students in an art school watching a painting being created. Their blank canvases about you are filling with color and shape as they grow up. Let the soft comfort of your compassion be splashed across the stretched white. May your abounding love be the circle drawn and your slow anger be a prominent theme. This is who you are as told to us in your Word. Let all other lies fade away from our minds. Sometimes, as their parents, we don't portray you accurately. May what they glean of you from us be true to who you are. As they discover who you are, let them fall deeply in love with you.

What does it mean to be quick to listen and slow to speak?

Anxiety

Lord, you are my shield,
My wonderful God who gives me courage.
I can lie down and go to sleep, and I will wake up again,
Because the Lord gives me strength.
Thousands of troops may surround me,
but I am not afraid.

Psalm 3:3, 5-6 ncv

"Don't let your hearts be troubled.
Trust in God, and trust also in me."

John 14:1 nlt

Give all your worries to him,
because he cares about you.

1 Peter 5:7 ncv

I was desperate for you to help me in my struggles,
and you did!

Psalm 120:1 tpt

Prince of peace, the very title of your name reassures us of who you are. You are the source of peace. Our children struggle with anxieties and worries sometimes, and it breaks our hearts. We want to lead them to your Word. We pray they will know that you will never leave them; they need not fear. May they understand that you take care of all our needs as our great provider. Let your presence comfort them and remove anxiety from them. May they learn to put their specific cares and worries into your loving hands. Let them be quick to turn to prayer. Give them the right words to say when something is bothering them. Cover them in your perfect peace and give them rest from what weighs on them. Thank you for all your promises.

What steps can you take to be less anxious and more trusting?

Beauty

I praise you because
you made me in an amazing
and wonderful way.
What you have done is wonderful.
I know this very well.

Psalm 139:14 ncv

Hold on to wisdom and good sense.
Don't let them out of your sight.
They will give you life
and beauty like a necklace around your neck.
Then you will go your way in safety,
and you will not get hurt.

Proverbs 3:21-23 ncv

God of the eternal, you have placed our family into this time and place in history. You have appointed us to parent these children. Where we are in life is not a shock or surprise to you. There is beauty to be found in our current season of parenting because you have designed it. Help us see it. For our children, you have placed eternity in their hearts. This means they feel the longing to be united with you. They know in their souls that they are made for something more. Give us the wisdom to encourage what is already inside of them. Please, reveal your will for their lives. Thank you for giving them purpose and meaning.

How can you see beauty
in your current season?

Blessings

Lord, how wonderfully you bless the righteous.
Your favor wraps around each one and covers them
under your canopy of kindness and joy.

PSALM 5:12 TPT

Surely you have granted him unending blessings
and made him glad with the joy of your presence.

PSALM 21:6 NIV

Every spiritual blessing in the heavenly realm has already
been lavished upon us as a love gift from our wonderful
heavenly Father, the Father of our Lord Jesus—all because
he sees us wrapped into Christ. This is why we celebrate
him with all our hearts! And in love he chose us before he
laid the foundation of the universe! Because of his great
love, he ordained us, so that we would be seen as holy in
his eyes with an unstained innocence.

EPHESIANS 1:3–4 TPT

Perfect Father, you never ignore the poor and needy. Help us to be more like you in this way. Thank you for the conviction to share our blessings from you. Give us generous hearts and help us cultivate the discipline of giving to others. Help us teach our children to be kind and extravagant givers. As you continue to provide for them and bless them with what they need, show them how to share those blessings with others. When selfishness rises up in our hearts, remind us that everything we have comes from you. Give us opportunities to share food with the hungry, to encourage the downtrodden, and to give whatever resources we have to those with less. May each person we encounter see a glimpse of who you are.

Which of God's blessings come to your mind today?

Boldness

He proclaimed the kingdom of God
and taught about the Lord Jesus Christ—
with all boldness and without hindrance!

Acts 28:31 niv

If an army surrounds me, I will not be afraid.
If war breaks out, I will trust the Lord.

Psalm 27:3 ncv

Let us come boldly to the throne of our gracious God.
There we will receive his mercy, and we will find grace
to help us when we need it most.

Hebrews 4:16 nlt

The wicked flee though no one pursues,
but the righteous are as bold as a lion.

Proverbs 28:1 niv

God who hears, it is because of your Son and his sacrifice that we have the boldness and confidence to approach your throne. Because of the blood of Jesus, we are clean. Thank you, Jesus, for interceding for us and knowing what we need. Even when we can't find the words, you are there. In parenting, we are often left without words. We don't even know what to pray for sometimes. Still, you know what is best for our family, and just coming before you and speaking your name is enough. In these situations, hear our intent and give us wisdom. We need your grace, patience, and perseverance. Give us each boldness to face each day and speak of your love to others.

Why is it sometimes hard to be bold?

Caring

Do not be interested only in your own life, but be
interested in the lives of others.

PHILIPPIANS 2:4 NCV

If anyone has material possessions and sees a brother or
sister in need but has no pity on them, how can the love
of God be in that person? Dear children, let us not love
with words or speech but with actions and in truth.

1 JOHN 3:17-18 NIV

"When you saw me hungry, you fed me. When you found
me thirsty, you gave me drink. When I had no place to
stay, you invited me in, and when I was poorly clothed,
you covered me. When I was sick, you tenderly cared for
me, and when I was in prison you visited me."
"Don't you know? When you cared for one of the least of
these, my little ones, my true brothers and sisters, you
demonstrated love for me."

MATTHEW 25:35-36, 40 TPT

God, you are wise, kind, and loving. You see the needs of our family and provide for us. We are without want. Thank you for taking care of us. As you take care of us, strengthen us to take good care of our kids. Help us not grumble and complain about meeting their physical needs. Help us to endure the mundane daily tasks required to raise children. Strengthen us to be vessels for them to bring nourishment to their souls and bodies. You have an abundant storehouse full of the things we daily need to parent. We ask for those things now. Caring for other people is an exhausting job. Will you refresh us? Our own strength, this world, and our relationships are wells that run dry quickly. You are good, and your provision is forever. Thank you for your care.

How can you care for
someone else today?

Change

Look! I tell you this secret:
We will not all sleep in death,
but we will all be changed.

1 Corinthians 15:51 ncv

He will take our weak mortal bodies and change them
into glorious bodies like his own, using the same power
with which he will bring everything under his control.

Philippians 3:21 nlt

Jesus Christ is the same yesterday
and today and forever.

Hebrews 13:8 niv

I will not be afraid, because the Lord is with me.
People can't do anything to me.

Psalm 118:6 ncv

Your promises are an anchor to our souls, God. We praise
you because you always are good on your word. You are who
you say you are, and your promises reveal your good character.
Whatever situations our children face, we pray you will teach
them to hold fast to your promises. When waves of trials crash
against them, may they find solid footing in your character
and on the fact that you never change. You will forever love
them. You will never leave them. You desire for them to be
saved, to know you, and to be in right relationship with you.
May your numerous promises bring them comfort. Give them
the ability to hide your Word inside of their hearts so that they
can recall your promises when other things are changing.

How do you handle change?

Children

Children are a gift from the LORD;
they are a reward from him.

"These words which I command you today shall be
in your heart. You shall teach them diligently to your
children, and shall talk of them when you sit in your
house, when you walk by the way, when you lie down,
and when you rise up."

"Let the little children come to Me, and do not forbid
them; for of such is the kingdom of heaven."

Direct your children onto the right path,
and when they are older, they will not leave it.

God who delivers us, you are the one who is mighty to save. You are the one whose strength is unmatched and who is omnipotent. We confess our desire to take on that role for our children. We want to save them, protect them, and keep them from all sorts of harm. They are a gift to us, and our instinct rises up to protect them. Give us wisdom to know when to swoop in and save and when to let them learn from the hardships that come their way. Let them set their hopes on you, that they will see you as the mighty Savior you are. You will always have their backs. Thank you for the blessing they are and for the opportunity to raise them under your care. Help us to continue to lead them to you as they grow in their own faith.

How can you show your children that they are a blessing today?

Compassion

When I am with those who are weak, I share their
weakness, for I want to bring the weak to Christ.
Yes, I try to find common ground with everyone,
doing everything I can to save some.

1 Corinthians 9:22 nlt

Have mercy on me, O God,
according to your unfailing love;
according to your great compassion
blot out my transgressions.

Psalm 51:1 niv

Praise be to the God and Father of our Lord Jesus Christ,
the Father of compassion and the God of all comfort.

2 Corinthians 1:3 niv

The Lord hears his people when they call to him for help.
He rescues them from all their troubles.

Psalm 34:17 nlt

Father God, this world can be a harsh place. It feels like there is no room for error. At home, we want to do our best as parents, but we mess up and disappoint people. Pressures from outside feel severe too. Will you wrap your arms around us? We know we are safe in your presence. No matter what we do, you are waiting to show compassion toward us. That's how great your love is. Help us to learn grace instead of striving to meet an impossible standard. In the same way, may we extend your compassion to our kids. We don't want to hold them to a standard they will never meet. Instead, let them run to us and recognize we are parents who understand. If we have been too overbearing on them, forgive us. We confess it to you and pray you will teach us the kind of compassion you so freely offer us.

How can you be a more compassionate person?

Confidence

Do not throw away your confidence,
which has a great reward.

HEBREWS 10:35 NCV

Be my rock of refuge,
to which I can always go;
give the command to save me,
for you are my rock and my fortress....
For you have been my hope, Sovereign LORD,
my confidence since my youth.

PSALM 71:3, 5 NIV

Perfect, absolute peace surrounds those
whose imaginations are consumed with you;
they confidently trust in you.

ISAIAH 26:3 TPT

God, a relationship with you brings quietness of spirit and confidence forever. We want our children to know that same security. We want them to follow you all their days. No matter the season they are in now, we ask you to deepen their faith in you. Meet them where they are and show them how much you love them. Draw them closer to you with your kindness and gently lead them to further repentance. Remind them that their righteousness is found in you. You are the one they look to for perfection. Seeking satisfaction and success in any other way will be fruitless and leave them wanting. May their lives be defined by having a quiet spirit and confidence in who they are because of what you have done on the cross.

How do you find your confidence?

Contentment

It is a good thing to receive wealth from God and the
good health to enjoy it. To enjoy your work and accept
your lot in life—this is indeed a gift from God.
God keeps such people so busy enjoying life
that they take no time to brood over the past.

ECCLESIASTES 5:19-20 NLT

I know what it is to be in need, and I know what it is to
have plenty. I have learned the secret of being content
in any and every situation, whether well fed or hungry,
whether living in plenty or in want. I can do all this
through him who gives me strength.

PHILIPPIANS 4:12-13 NIV

Those that the LORD has rescued will return. They will
enter Zion with singing; everlasting joy will crown their
heads. Gladness and joy will overtake them,
and sorrow and sighing will flee away.

ISAIAH 35:10 NIV

Jesus, you are the living water. You offer yourself to us with the tantalizing promise of never thirsting again. When we drink deeply from the fountain of salvation, you fill us with joy. This is a satisfying and long-lasting joy that can always be found when one enters your presence. Happiness is fleeting, yet that is often what the world chases. Let our kids know the difference. Keep them from the fruitless pursuit of happiness and instead set them on the path to joy. Let them see how temporary happiness is and how your joy will sustain them through anything they face. Let them drink deeply. Thank you for providing for us in this way. You satisfy us and bring contentment to our souls.

How can you choose to be content with your life as it is right now?

Courage

Be strong in the Lord and in his mighty power.
Put on the full armor of God, so that you can
take your stand against the devil's schemes.

Ephesians 6:10-11 NIV

Be alert. Continue strong in the faith.
Have courage, and be strong. Do everything in love.

1 Corinthians 16:13-14 NCV

Even though I walk through the darkest valley,
I will fear no evil, for you are with me;
your rod and your staff, they comfort me.

Psalm 23:4 NIV

"This is my command—be strong and courageous!
Do not be afraid or discouraged. For the Lord
your God is with you wherever you go."

Joshua 1:9 NLT

Jesus, we ask you to give our children hearts of courage.
When they feel fear, when they experience the troubles and the
sorrows you spoke of, give them peace based on your presence.
Let them know you will never leave them or forsake them. Give
them confidence as they do the work you have prepared for
them. Teach them to also rest from their work; let their souls
find rest in you alone. Give them a desire to follow your ways.
Give them courage to act on your Word and do the right thing
when faced with adversity. Let them be rebellious against
fear and timidity and full of strength to walk in the opposite
direction of a world that is walking toward its destruction.
In all this courage, let them not find their worth in being the
strong one or the brave one but in being yours. Remind them
that this bravery only comes from the power of your Spirit.

When was the last time
you asked God for courage?

Courtesy

Each of us should please our neighbors for their good,
to build them up. For even Christ did not please himself
but, as it is written: "The insults of those who
insult you have fallen on me."

Romans 15:2-3 niv

Remind people to respect their governmental leaders
on every level as law-abiding citizens and to be ready to
fulfill their civic duty. And remind them to never tear
down anyone with their words or quarrel, but instead be
considerate, humble, and courteous to everyone.

Titus 3:1-2 tpt

Welcome strangers, because some who have done this
have welcomed angels without knowing it.

Hebrews 13:2 ncv

Perfect Father, thank you for the love you shower on us. Give our children a revelation of the love that you have for them. As they experience your love, help them to love others well. Open their eyes to see the needs of others. Teach them to put the needs of others before their own. Soften their hearts toward those in need. Give them spirits of humility so they will never look down on anyone who has less than they do. Give them opportunities to serve those around them. As they refresh others, you will refresh them. If they do not grow weary of doing good, they will reap a harvest of righteousness. Give them perseverance in love. May they lean on you as their source so that they can give abundantly like you do. Keep them connected to you, and may they continuously be courteous of others.

Why is it sometimes difficult to place the needs of your children before your own?

Creativity

We are God's masterpiece.
He has created us anew in Christ Jesus,
so we can do the good things he planned for us long ago.
EPHESIANS 2:10 NLT

He has filled him with the Spirit of God,
with wisdom, with understanding,
with knowledge and with all kinds of skills.
EXODUS 35:31 NIV

We have different gifts,
according to the grace given to each of us.
ROMANS 12:6 NIV

LORD, you have made many things;
with your wisdom you made them all.
The earth is full of your riches.
PSALM 104:24 NCV

Creative God, you have made a tapestry of peoples. There is endless beauty to be found in the wide variety of ethnicities and cultures spread among the nations. You do not show partiality to one particular people; all who come to you are accepted by you. Let our family mirror your heart in this manner. Search our hearts and reveal if there is any partiality toward excluding some and elevating others. Help us not cling to the familiar and seek out faces that reflect our own. Instead, may we love all people well. The pride in our hearts brings bias and prejudice. We confess this sin to you and ask that you show us a new way. Help us guide our children in this path as we celebrate and rejoice in your image that you so vibrantly displayed in humankind. Thank you for the gift of creativity. Help us teach our children how to use it in their lives.

How can you use your creativity for God?

Delight

When your words came, I ate them;
they were my joy and my heart's delight,
for I bear your name,
Lord God Almighty.

JEREMIAH 15:16 NIV

"My God, I want to do what you want.
Your teachings are in my heart."

PSALM 40:8 NCV

Your laws are my treasure;
they are my heart's delight.

PSALM 119:111 NLT

"Let your light shine before others, that they may see
your good deeds and glorify your Father in heaven."

MATTHEW 5:16 NIV

Jesus, you are the way, the truth, and the life. In your presence, there is endless joy to be found. We want our children to know your delight as well. As they grow up, let them find you to be the way. There are many ways presented in this world, but nothing satisfies like you do. Give them the wisdom to discern between paths that lead to sin and death and paths that lead to you. Let them taste of the sweet joy that comes from knowing you. We pray they will crave your ways and find delight in what your heart delights in. Let us be an example of those who follow your ways. Let them see us seeking your will and your face. Thank you for pursuing our hearts and bringing us to you. Please do the same with our children and show them your delight.

How hard is it for you to fathom God's incredible delight in you?

Depression

Why am I so sad? Why am I so upset?
I should put my hope in God
and keep praising him.

PSALM 42:11 NCV

You, O LORD, are a shield about me,
my glory, and the lifter of my head.

PSALM 3:3 ESV

He has delivered us from the power of darkness and
conveyed us into the kingdom of the Son of His love.

COLOSSIANS 1:13 NKJV

"I am Yahweh, your mighty God!
I grip your right hand and won't let you go!
I whisper to you:
'Don't be afraid; I am here to help you!'"

ISAIAH 41:13 TPT

God, the curse brought death, sadness, and pain. These things make us feel hopeless when we face them with our power. What can we, lowly humans, do to remove pain from the lives of our children? We try to shield them as best we can, but ultimately, we fall short. You, mighty Father, have conquered sin and death through your Son. You are compassionate toward us, and we thank you for that. Since you have conquered death, we need not be subject to the old ways anymore. This fills us with joyous hope and brings us out of our depression. When our children face the troubles of the world, help us communicate your hope to them. Let them know that they too can be free from the chains of sadness and grief.

Can you sense God's comfort and joy in the middle of your sadness today?

Devotion

Then Jesus said to his disciples, "Whoever wants
to be my disciple must deny themselves and
take up their cross and follow me."

MATTHEW 16:24 NIV

"No servant can serve two masters. The servant will hate
one master and love the other, or will follow one master
and refuse to follow the other. You cannot serve
both God and worldly riches."

LUKE 16:13 NCV

Don't copy the behavior and customs of this world, but
let God transform you into a new person by changing the
way you think. Then you will learn to know God's will
for you, which is good and pleasing and perfect.

ROMANS 12:2 NLT

Dear God, you are the most perfect father our children will ever have. You know them inside and out. You are aware of all their comings and goings, and you have their days memorized. You love them with an everlasting love. Our devotion and love for them can't compare to your faithfulness and love. You have given us the gift of being their parents, so teach us to surrender them back to you in everything we do. Help us to loosen our grasp and remember that we can't control every aspect of their lives. We want to lean on you and trust you. Teach us how to trust you fully. When things happen in our family that we don't understand, help us to rely on you instead of ourselves. Your understanding is thorough, and your wisdom is great. We surrender our family wholly to you. Help us to be devoted to you every day.

How can you devote your life more to God?

Encouragement

"The Lord your God is with you;
the mighty One will save you.
He will rejoice over you. You will rest in his love;
he will sing and be joyful about you."

ZEPHANIAH 3:17 NCV

Encourage one another daily,
as long as it is called "Today."

HEBREWS 3:13 NIV

Kind words are like honey—
sweet to the soul and healthy for the body.

PROVERBS 16:24 NLT

Be joyful. Grow to maturity. Encourage each other.
Live in harmony and peace.
Then the God of love and peace will be with you.

2 CORINTHIANS 13:11 NLT

God, we have experienced your strength. On many occasions, you have lifted us up on wings like an eagle's, and you have renewed our strength when we didn't think we could go any further. When we have been discouraged, you have brought us new life. We have known your faithfulness, and we ask that you reveal that same faithfulness to our children. May the testimony of our lives be an encouragement to them of how much you love your children. Strengthen them for the journey ahead. May they look to you for strength all their days. May they lean on you in their weakness and trust that you will help them run without being weary. You will renew them, and as they follow you, you will guide each and every step that they take.

How can you encourage
someone today?

Enthusiasm

Whatever you do, work heartily,
as for the Lord and not for men,
knowing that from the Lord you will
receive the inheritance as your reward.
You are serving the Lord Christ.

<small>COLOSSIANS 3:23–24 ESV</small>

"When I discovered your words, I devoured them.
They are my joy and my heart's delight,
for I bear your name,
O LORD God of Heaven's Armies."

<small>JEREMIAH 15:16 NLT</small>

Make the most of every opportunity.
Let your conversation be always full of grace.

<small>COLOSSIANS 4:5–6 NIV</small>

Almighty God, the way you have always been the one who rides in on the white horse to save us is breathtaking. We have never lived a moment where your heart and your plan has not been the very best. We want to fully understand and own how you have moved on our behalf, so we can offer up not only our thanksgiving but our lives. We want our children to grow up in a home that is filled with your Spirit and where you reign supreme. We pray they will be so engulfed with excitement over your love and protection for them that their praises raise up to you as a sweet aroma. May they go forward confidently in life knowing that your grace, care, and provision will always guide and follow them. Give them enthusiasm to walk with you all of their lives.

How can you show enthusiasm for the season you are in right now?

Eternity

We are citizens of heaven,
where the Lord Jesus Christ lives.
And we are eagerly waiting for him to return as our Savior.

Philippians 3:20 nlt

"If I go and prepare a place for you, I will come back and
take you to be with me that you also may be where I am."

John 14:3 niv

It will happen in an instant—in the twinkling of his eye.
For when the last trumpet is sounded, the dead will come
back to life. We will be indestructible and we will be
transformed.

1 Corinthians 15:52 tpt

Surely your goodness and love will be with me all my life,
and I will live in the house of the Lord forever.

Psalm 23:6 ncv

God, we praise you for who you are. You are the great Creator who has made a way for his children to be reunited with him and given us a kingdom that is everlasting. This is amazing! Let our children know the truth about you and worship you. Develop in them the spirit of worship that is not pointed in any direction other than at you. Let them live their days in awe of you as they notice your fingerprints all over creation and long for the age to come. Let their hope lie firmly in eternity and in the promise you have given us. Let your praise ring from their lips; may they never be silent. Develop a spirit of gratitude in them. May they see you as the source of their lives and salvation and be humbly grateful.

Can you view eternity with a hopeful, happy heart, fully trusting in a good God?

Excellence

Finally, brothers and sisters, whatever is true, whatever
is noble, whatever is right, whatever is pure, whatever is
lovely, whatever is admirable—if anything is excellent or
praiseworthy—think about such things.

Philippians 4:8 niv

By his divine power, God has given us everything we
need for living a godly life. We have received all of this by
coming to know him, the one who called us to himself
by means of his marvelous glory and excellence.

2 Peter 1:3 nlt

The answer is, if you eat or drink, or if you do anything,
do it all for the glory of God.

1 Corinthians 10:31 ncv

We praise you, God, for drawing us to yourself. You call us to wake from the sleep that leads to death. Thank you for the opportunity to be known by you and called your own. There are areas of parenting where we know we are coming up short. We are at the end of our own wisdom regarding so many things. Can you provide wisdom? You have called us to this role of parent, and we want to be excellent in it. Please give us what we need to fulfill the job. Even when we are unsure of what to ask for or unsure of what we need, we come to you because we know you are faithful to provide in abundance.

In which areas would you like to be excellent for God?

Faith

"I promise you, if you have faith inside of you no bigger
than the size of a small mustard seed, you can say to this
mountain, 'Move away from here and go over there,' and
you will see it move. There is nothing you couldn't do!"

MATTHEW 17:20 TPT

Since we have been made right in God's sight by faith,
we have peace with God because of what Jesus Christ
our Lord has done for us.

ROMANS 5:1 NLT

The important thing is faith—
the kind of faith that works through love.

GALATIANS 5:6 NCV

Faith is confidence in what we hope for
and assurance about what we do not see.

HEBREWS 11:1 NIV

God, we pray for the next generation. We ask that this
generation, the one we are helping to shape, will be a
mountain-moving generation of faith. Please build in them
great faith. Let this be their legacy. May they be a generation
that asks for mountains to be moved. When they look, they
will not focus on the height and width of the mountain in
front of them but on your greatness. Let them be like David,
who when faced with Goliath asked, "Who is this that defies
the armies of the living God?" May that be their motto:
what is this that defies God. Then, may they boldly battle.
Arm them with your armor and reward their faith. Let their
generation see the sick healed, many come to salvation in
your name, and revival of your Spirit. Take their little faith
and do great things with it. We know you will do great things
in the lives of our children.

What gives you faith and hope in Jesus?

Faithfulness

Your mercy, Lord, extends to the heavens,
Your faithfulness reaches to the skies.

Psalm 36:5 nasb

Lord, you are my God;
I will exalt you and praise your name,
for in perfect faithfulness you have done wonderful
things, things planned long ago.

Isaiah 25:1 niv

The word of the Lord is upright,
and all his work is done in faithfulness.

Psalm 33:4 esv

The Lord is faithful, who will establish you
and guard you from the evil one.

2 Thessalonians 3:3 nkjv

You are perfect in all your ways, God. The eternal nature of your mercy astounds us. As you are faithful, can you develop faithfulness in us? When we are tempted to respond in impatience and irritation toward our children, will you help us to be faithful to love them instead? You love us unconditionally. In the mundane moments of parenting, help us remain faithful. Sometimes, things are not hard; they are just boring. Cooking dinner again, reading them the same book again, driving the same route to a particular activity again. But you have called us here to parent, so help us to be faithful to the task at hand. Give us the creativity to connect with our children in new ways. May we continue to pursue and love them well even when we want to check out. Great is your faithfulness, oh Lord, and the example you set for us.

How have you seen the faithfulness of God in your life?

Family

"Choose for yourselves this day whom you will serve...
as for me and my household, we will serve the Lord."

Joshua 24:15 niv

Her children arise and call her blessed;
her husband also, and he praises her.

Proverbs 31:28 niv

For this reason I bow my knees before the Father,
from whom every family in heaven and
on earth derives its name.

Ephesians 3:14-15 nasb

One of the deepest desires of the human heart is to belong. Thank you, Father, for making us your children. You chose us, and we belong to you. You truly want us, and that blows our minds. Being our Father brings you pleasure. We confess we sometimes forget the truth of our secure identity as your children. Will you remind us? Thank you for the gift of our earthly children. Each of them is unique and precious. When things are hard, remind us that they are a gift. Stir up in our hearts the things you love about them. Show us how to love them well. We pray they will find belonging and safety in your family. Give us wisdom to reassure them of their eternal value.

How can you treasure your family today?

Fear

God will never give you the spirit of fear, but the Holy
Spirit who gives you might power, love, and self-control.

2 Timothy 1:7 tpt

The Lord is my light and my salvation—
whom shall I fear?
The Lord is the stronghold of my life—
of whom shall I be afraid?

Psalm 27:1 niv

When I am afraid, I will trust you.
I praise God for his word.
I trust God, so I am not afraid.
What can human beings do to me?

Psalm 56:3-4 ncv

Good Father, you tell us in your Word that your perfect love drives out fear. You do not want us to be afraid or live under that bondage. In your goodness, you have given us ways to be free from fear. Please, remove any influence of fear over our children. Replace its presence with your good presence. Let love and peace fill their souls instead. Give them the bravery they need to face their fears. Let them know you fight for them, you are near to them, and you will never leave them. In the midst of a scary situation, let your overwhelming love flood the moment and change the atmosphere. We trust that you love them deeply and will give them true freedom from fear.

What fears can you give
to God right now?

Forgiveness

He is so rich in kindness and grace that he purchased our
freedom with the blood of his Son and forgave our sins.

EPHESIANS 1:7 NLT

As far as the east is from the west,
So far has He removed our wrongdoings from us.

PSALM 103:12 NASB

If we confess our sins, He is faithful and just to forgive us
our sins and to cleanse us from all unrighteousness.

1 JOHN 1:9 NKJV

"If you forgive other people when they sin against you,
your heavenly Father will also forgive you."

MATTHEW 6:14 NIV

Heavenly Father, in you is perfect love. Draw our children closer to you to know that perfect love. As they experience your selflessness and perfection, teach them to love others the same way. May they be so firmly rooted in your love that they are unshaken by the actions of others. May their confidence and security come first from you. May your steadfast love give them the courage to love boldly. When they are hurt, may they run to you for comfort. As you mend what is broken, fill them with love that overflows to those around them. Holy Spirit, give them the grace to forgive and to return hurt with love and kindness. Teach them how to be slow to anger and quick to forgive. May their hearts reflect yours, and may their actions draw others closer to you. In our family, may we all display forgiveness in a way that honors you.

Who might you need to
extend forgiveness to today?

Friendship

A friend loves you all the time,
and a brother helps in time of trouble.

PROVERBS 17:17 NCV

There are "friends" who destroy each other,
but a real friend sticks closer than a brother.

PROVERBS 18:24 NLT

"Greater love has no one than this: to lay down one's life
for one's friends. You are my friends if you do
what I command.... Instead, I have called you friends,
for everything that I learned from my Father
I have made known to you."

JOHN 15:13-15 NIV

"In everything, do to others
what you would have them to do to you."

MATTHEW 7:12 NIV

Jesus, in your Word, you say that we are your friends. You call those who believe in you no longer servants but friends. What a wonderful truth! You are the friend who sticks closest and demonstrates great love toward us. May our kids know you as a friend. May they have that special relationship and intimacy with you. We pray also for their earthly friendships. Please, surround them with wise people. May their friendships be like iron sharpening iron, and may they influence each other to be better friends and closer to you. Remind them to be loyal and loving. Build up good qualities in them and bless them with good friendships all their lives.

What friends spur you on in your relationship with God?

Generosity

"Give generously to them and do so without a grudging heart; then because of this the LORD your God will bless you in all your work and in everything you put your hand to."

DEUTERONOMY 15:10 NIV

Let giving flow from your heart, not from a sense of religious duty. Let it spring up freely from the joy of giving—all because God loves hilarious generosity!

2 CORINTHIANS 9:7 TPT

If you help the poor, you are lending to the LORD— and he will repay you!

PROVERBS 19:17 NLT

God of abundance, your riches stretch farther than our wildest imaginations. We praise you for all you offer. We don't have to live in fear or wonder if there will be enough. You promise to care for us and provide for us. Thank you for being a good father in this manner. We pray our kids will not be burdened by the weight of scarcity. May they not cling to material things, money, talents, or wisdom that you bestow on them, but may they use them for your glory. May they serve and give generously without reserve like cups that pour out only to be filled up again and again. When they are moved to be generous to others, don't let us hold them back. Unfurl our clinging hands as we learn to walk in your kingdom way.

How do you feel when you share with others?

Gentleness

"Accept my teachings and learn from me,
because I am gentle and humble in spirit,
and you will find rest for your lives."

MATTHEW 11:29 NCV

"What blessing comes to you
when gentleness lives in you!
For you will inherit the earth."

MATTHEW 5:5 TPT

A gentle answer turns away wrath,
but a harsh word stirs up anger.

PROVERBS 15:1 NIV

He is able to deal gently with those who are ignorant and
are going astray, since he himself is subject to weakness.

HEBREWS 5:2 NIV

Father, we are not naturally full of mercy as you are. We praise you for extending such lavish grace on us. Teach our family to forgive others as you forgive. Fill us with grace and mercy. Let us learn to be gentle with those around us. Upon receiving your mercy, let it flow out of us. When others wrong us, don't let bitterness, revenge, or anger take root in our hearts. Instead, remind us that you are the one who defends us. When we want to retaliate, give us self-control instead. Help us leave everything at the foot of the cross. Increase our capacity for love and gentleness toward others. Thank you for the example you set for us.

What are some steps you can take to become more gentle?

Goodness

Everything God created is good, and nothing is to be
rejected if it is received with thanksgiving.

1 Timothy 4:4 niv

Taste and see that the Lord is good.
Oh, the joys of those who take refuge in him!

Psalm 34:8 nlt

I remain confident of this:
I will see the goodness of the Lord
in the land of the living.

Psalm 27:13 niv

They will tell about the amazing things you do,
and I will tell how great you are.
They will remember your great goodness
and will sing about your fairness.

Psalm 145:6-7 ncv

God of creation, we see the work of your hands in the heavens above. The way you made and govern the sun, moon, and stars inspires awe in us. Their purpose and beauty teach us about your character. You made all creation: the snow drifting through the sky, the wildflowers blooming in the spring, the summer fireflies, and the fall leaves. You are good. You are beautiful. Your generosity with beauty in our world reminds us that you are benevolent in your goodness toward us. May our kids know this goodness and beauty. When they interact with creation, may it raise their curiosity for you. Let wonder reign in their imaginings about you. Let your praise be on their lips all the days of their lives for the goodness you bestow on them.

Where do you see the goodness of God the most in your life?

Grace

Indeed, we have all received grace upon grace
from his fullness.

JOHN 1:16 CSB

God gives us even more grace,
as the Scripture says, "God is against the proud,
but he gives grace to the humble."

JAMES 4:6 NCV

Sin is no longer your master, for you no longer live
under the requirements of the law. Instead, you live
under the freedom of God's grace.

ROMANS 6:14 NLT

Christ gave each one of us the special gift of grace,
showing how generous he is.

EPHESIANS 4:7 NCV

God, we are so grateful that we are saved by grace alone.
We ask for grace over our children's lives. May they come to
the knowledge of your saving grace and apply it daily. Help
them not to get caught up in striving for works to prove their
righteousness; may they rest in your grace. As they rest, let it
be by the power of your Holy Spirit that their deeds bring you
glory. Let them operate out of this place of strength as they do
things for your glory and enact good deeds because you help
them. Let them live in balance. Keep them from a life of works
and striving to gain your affection. Your affection is already
won. Thank you for your grace.

What does God's grace look like
in your life?

Grief

Those who sow in tears shall reap with shouts of joy.

PSALM 126:5 ESV

May your faithful love comfort me
as you promised your servant.

PSALM 119:76 CSB

"Come to me, all you who are weary and burdened,
and I will give you rest. Take my yoke upon you
and learn from me, for I am gentle and humble in heart,
and you will find rest for your souls."

MATTHEW 11:28-29 NIV

"Every valley shall be raised up,
every mountain and hill made low;
the rough ground shall become level,
the rugged places a plain."

ISAIAH 40:4 NIV

Heavenly Father, thank you for never leaving us alone in our grief. Thank you for promising compassion. When we walk through seasons of grief as parents, help us turn to you. May your promises be at the forefront of our mind; may our instinct be to remember what you have said. Help us to rest in your presence and turn to you for comfort instead of to worldly substitutes. We want to find safety and security in your love no matter what we are grieving. When we are helping our children walk through grief, may we point them to you. Give us the right words to bring comfort and encouragement. Give us discernment to know when to speak and when to stay silent. Teach us how to walk alongside them with compassion and tenderness.

Do you ask God for help when you need his comfort?

Guidance

Guide me in your truth and teach me,
for you are God my Savior,
and my hope is in you all day long.

Psalm 25:5 niv

I praise the Lord because he advises me.
Even at night, I feel his leading.
I keep the Lord before me always.
Because he is close by my side,
I will not be hurt.

Psalm 16:7-8 ncv

We can make our plans,
but the Lord determines our steps.

Proverbs 16:9 nlt

Those who are led by the Spirit of God
are children of God.

Romans 8:14 niv

Heavenly Father, why do we revert to frantically and insufficiently concocting our own solutions to difficulties when we know that you already have it handled. Please help us stop dead in our tracks whenever we try to plot our own plan. Make our first and foremost response to be to run to you and let us do it in clear view of our children. We pray they always seek you first. We ask that they have absolute trust in your will and your ways for them. Let them never solely carry the anxiety of life's unpleasant or tragic surprises; help them know without a shadow of a doubt that you have gone before them and answered their prayers before they even approach you. Help them seek all their wisdom, comfort, protection, and guidance from you.

Is there anything God can help guide you in today?

Guilt

If we confess our sins, he is faithful and just
and will forgive us our sins and purify us
from all unrighteousness.

1 John 1:9 niv

Because the Sovereign Lord helps me,
I will not be disgraced,
Therefore have I set my face like flint,
and I know I will not be put to shame.

Isaiah 50:7 niv

Those who go to him for help are happy,
and they are never disgraced.

Psalm 34:5 ncv

I have not achieved it, but I focus on this one thing:
Forgetting the past and looking forward
to what lies ahead.

Philippians 3:13 nlt

God, when the past rears its ugly head, taunting us to feel shame and guilt over old sins, we desperately want to shut it down immediately. You have forgiven us. We are so thankful that you saved us from our dark and wicked ways. We pray our children will come to know you and be transformed into your likeness at an early age. Give them the power of your Holy Spirit to say no to sin the minute it entices them. Let them have wisdom and discernment to know good from evil, that they would be known for their righteousness. When they come to you and confess, give them assurance of your forgiveness, and take away their guilt. Help them to live a life that points to and glorifies you.

Why doesn't God want you
to feel guilt and shame?

Health

The world and its desires pass away,
but whoever does the will of God lives forever.

1 JOHN 2:17 NIV

Do not be wise in your own eyes;
Fear the LORD and shun evil.
This will bring health to your body
and nourishment to your bones.

PROVERBS 3:7-8 NIV

I will never forget your commandments,
for by them you give me life.

PSALM 119:93 NLT

A happy heart is like good medicine,
but a broken spirit drains your strength.

PROVERBS 17:22 NCV

We praise you, God, for you are in control and sovereign over our world. When our sight is clouded by frustration or fear, reveal the goodness you are growing in our kids' lives. Use us in their lives; don't let us get in the way of the good plans you have for them. Keep after them, drawing their hearts closer to you all their days. Bless them with health— mentally, physically, emotionally, and spiritually. Help them to thrive in the good works that you have planned for them. We pray their hearts will be soft for your discipline and receptive to repentance. When we are feeling nervous about their lives, remind us of this truth: you are mighty, and you are working.

What healing are you believing God for right now?

Helpfulness

"In everything I did, I showed you that by
this kind of hard work we must help the weak,
remembering the words the Lord Jesus himself said:
'It is more blessed to give than to receive.'"

Acts 20:35 niv

"Who is greater, the one who is at the table or the one
who serves? Is it not the one who is at the table?
But I am among you as one who serves."

Luke 22:27 tpt

Share with God's people who need help.
Bring strangers in need into your homes.

Romans 12:13 ncv

God, thank you for the passions you have put inside our children. We are grateful that you are going to use them to do great things for your kingdom. Let their lives be testimonies of your faithfulness. As they interact with the world around them, help them resist outrage and argument. Let them be different. May they lead with patience and kindness, helping others with no desire for selfish gain. Give them gentle wisdom to know how to fight for those who are oppressed and to seek true justice in your name. Thank you for the hearts and passions you have put inside them. Fan into flame their gifts and their character even more. Give them helpful hearts and strength to serve others in ways that draw people to you.

What is something helpful you could do for someone today?

Honesty

Keep me from deceitful ways;
be gracious to me and teach me your law.

PSALM 119:29 NIV

The king is pleased with words from righteous lips;
he loves those who speak honestly.

PROVERBS 16:13 NLT

Instead we will remain strong and always sincere in
our love as we express the truth. All our direction and
ministries will flow from Christ and lead us deeper into
him, the anointed Head of his body, the church.

EPHESIANS 4:15 TPT

"Everything that is hidden will become clear,
and every secret thing will be made known."

LUKE 8:17 NCV

God, we know that you want us to live in the light. You don't want us to live in lies, shame, or condemnation. Instead, you've told us to confess our sins to each other and give our burdens to you. Help us do this regularly in our home. We don't want to cultivate pride or selfishness. We want to set a standard of honest communication and a willingness to admit when we are wrong. Teach us how to be peacemakers. Remind us to pray for each other, and may we listen when the Holy Spirit leads us toward confession. Soften our hearts to hear your voice and give us the grace to respond to conviction.

Is there anything you need to be honest about now?

Hope

The LORD is good to those whose hope is in him,
to the one who seeks him.

LAMENTATIONS 3:25 NIV

This hope is not a disappointing fantasy, because we can
now experience the endless love of God cascading into
our hearts through the Holy Spirit who lives in us!

ROMANS 5:5 TPT

God has given both his promise and his oath. These two
things are unchangeable because it is impossible for God
to lie. Therefore, we who have fled to him for refuge can
have great confidence as we hold to the hope that lies
before us. This hope is a strong and trustworthy anchor
for our souls. It leads us through the curtain into
God's inner sanctuary.

HEBREWS 6:18-19 NLT

Heavenly Father, thank you for the hope we have found in Christ's promised return. Open our children's eyes to this hope. Draw them to you at a young age and give them the grace to respond. Teach them who you are and how much you love them. May they be firmly and deeply rooted in your love. No matter where life takes them, may the hope of Christ's return always overflow from their hearts. May they be sustained by that great hope. When they are discouraged, may they draw strength from the fact that you will never leave them or forsake them, and you are coming back again.

Knowing that God always hears you,
what can you be hopeful for?

Humility

"My hand made these things so they all belong to me,"
declares Yahweh.
"But there is one my eyes are drawn to:
the humble one, the tender one,
the trembling one
who lives in awe of all I say."

ISAIAH 66:2 TPT

Pride will ruin people,
but those who are humble will be honored.

PROVERBS 29:23 NCV

"The LORD has told you what is good,
and this is what he requires of you:
to do what is right, to love mercy,
and to walk humbly with your God."

MICAH 6:8 NLT

Perfect Father, we know that we make mistakes often.
We know that we need your perfection to cover us. Please
soften our hearts. Help us maintain an attitude of humility.
Especially with our children, we want to be quick to recognize
our mistakes and quick to ask for forgiveness. When we do the
wrong thing, help us to seek restitution in a way that honors
you and prioritizes our kids. In times when we are stubborn
or selfish, lead us back to you with kindness. May we never be
too proud for correction or too frustrated to seek healing in our
relationships. We want to be a model for our children of how
to put the needs of others before personal gain. We know that
as we embrace humility, you will take care of all we need.

What opportunities give you a chance
to practice humility today?

Inspiration

The precepts of the LORD are right,
giving joy to the heart.
The commands of the LORD are radiant,
giving light to the eyes.

PSALM 19:8 NIV

Your laws are my treasure;
they are my heart's delight.

PSALM 119:111 NLT

God has transmitted his very substance into every
Scripture, for it is God-breathed. It will empower you
by its instruction and correction, giving you
the strength to take the right direction
and lead you deeper into the path of godliness.

2 TIMOTHY 3:16 TPT

God who is not hidden from us, we praise you. You make it easy to be in your presence. All creation is covered in your visible fingerprints; one doesn't even have to dust for them. Thank you for the natural curiosity you put inside our children. Their desire to learn and their love for life is inspirational. Let their curiosity grow and lead them to you. When they encounter the created world, let it spark questions in them about you, their Creator. You will answer them, and they will find you. Thank you for this promise.

How do you find inspiration?

Integrity

I know, my God, that you test the heart and
are pleased with integrity. All these things
I have given willingly and with honest intent.

1 Chronicles 29:17 niv

"So if you ignore the least commandment and teach others
to do the same, you will be called the least in the Kingdom
of Heaven. But anyone who obeys God's laws and teaches
them will be called great in the Kingdom of Heaven."

Matthew 5:19 nlt

The honest person will live in safety,
but the dishonest will be caught.

Proverbs 10:9 ncv

Perfect King, you always have integrity. You never stray from the truth, and your righteousness has no end. We are fickle. We are prone to protect ourselves instead of always living with integrity. Strengthen our children's resolve. Give them a deep desire for honesty. Even when it's hard, help them to tell the truth while knowing that you will uphold them. Cultivate within them the discipline of being honest no matter how uncomfortable it is. May they value integrity more than they value their own comfort. Soften their hearts toward you so that when they make mistakes, they will run to you instead of walking away in shame.

Do you admire the integrity
of someone in your life?

Joy

May the God of hope fill you with all joy and peace
as you trust in him, so that you may overflow
with hope by the power of the Holy Spirit.

ROMANS 15:13 NIV

"Don't be sad, because the joy of the LORD
will make you strong."

NEHEMIAH 8:10 NCV

The LORD is my strength and shield.
I trust him with all my heart.
He helps me, and my heart is filled with joy.
I burst out in songs of thanksgiving.

PSALM 28:7 NLT

Be cheerful with joyous celebration in every
season of life. Let your joy overflow!

PHILIPPIANS 4:4 TPT

Turn our hearts to remember you today, God. As the days go on in a sometimes monotonous procession of work, chores, and the needs of kids, we confess we lose joy. We take for granted how glorious of a truth it is that you are trustworthy to save. You have brought us out of the kingdom of death and into your kingdom of life! Refresh our spirits. Grant us new joy in our salvation. Let this joy be contagious in our household; may those who live with us join in praising you. Let spontaneous praise and rejoicing break out. Let us see your marvelous deeds in creation and give you praise. Warm our hearts and fill them with joy. Help us share your joy with those around us.

What is one truly joyful moment you've had recently?

Justice

He would never crush a broken heart nor disregard
the weak and vulnerable. He will make sure justice
comes to those who are wronged.

ISAIAH 42:3 TPT

Beloved, do not avenge yourselves,
but rather give place to wrath; for it is written,
"Vengeance is Mine, I will repay," says the Lord.

ROMANS 12:19 NKJV

He did not retaliate when he was insulted,
nor threaten revenge when he suffered.
He left his case in the hands of God,
who always judges fairly.

1 PETER 2:23 NLT

God of justice, all your ways are right and good. You have worked to defend and uphold the oppressed and the weak since the fall of man. You care deeply for those who society casts aside. May our children be children who seek justice. Let them have hearts of compassion for the needy, the poor, and the marginalized on our earth. We pray they will fight for justice and stand up against the bullies of this world. Put these passions inside of them. Give them clarity when they are trying to discern the right thing to do. Let them know it in their bones. Protect them as you raise them up as seekers of justice. When they see the pain of the world, let it create empathy. Shield their hearts from becoming hard. Instead, let their hearts be set on fire to join you on your mission.

Why is it better to let
God be the judge?

Kindness

Be kind to each other, tenderhearted, forgiving one another, just as God through Christ has forgiven you.

EPHESIANS 4:32 NLT

Kind people do themselves a favor,
but cruel people bring trouble on themselves.

PROVERBS 11:17 NCV

Do the riches of his extraordinary kindness make you take him for granted and despise him? Haven't you experienced how kind and understanding he has been to you? Don't mistake his tolerance for acceptance. Do you realize that all the wealth of his extravagant kindness is meant to melt your heart and lead you into repentance?

ROMANS 2:4 TPT

Gentle God, you describe yourself as kind. We praise you for your kindness and your humility. We want to know your kindness. We repent of the incorrect ways we have viewed you. Free us from all the incorrect boxes we have tried to place you in and bring us clarity of sight to experience who you are. Let our children know you as kind and loving. May they be free from the blinders that the world tries to put on them. May they know there is a God who is madly in love with them, pursuing them, and ready to extend abundant mercy toward them. Help our parenting reflect this glorious truth: you are kind.

How can you extend kindness
to those around you today?

Loneliness

"Teach them to obey everything that I have taught you,
and I will be with you always,
even until the end of this age."

Matthew 28:20 ncv

The Lord is near to all who call on him,
yes, to all who call on him in truth.

Psalm 145:18 nlt

Even if my father and mother abandon me,
the Lord will hold me close.

Psalm 27:10 nlt

"Be strong and courageous. Do not be afraid or terrified
because of them, for the Lord your God goes with you;
he will never leave you nor forsake you."

Deuteronomy 31:6 niv

Blessed King, we are not worthy of your goodness, your kindness, or your gentleness. You are mighty and powerful, yet you call us yours. You are righteous and perfect, yet you redeem us when we don't deserve it. Give our children a revelation of who you are and how great your love is for them. They are called by you. Show them that they are yours. When they feel lonely or like they don't belong, open their eyes to see that belonging is found in you. You are the only one who can set them free. You redeem them and give them a strong foundation. Soften their hearts toward you. As they turn to you, give them confidence in who they are. May your love cast out all fear in their hearts. May they walk confidently in the knowledge that they are part of your family and that they are never alone.

When you feel lonely,
can you turn to God?

Love

Three things will last forever—
faith, hope, and love—
and the greatest of these is love.

1 Corinthians 13:13 nlt

Fill us with your love every morning.
Then we will sing and rejoice all our lives.

Psalm 90:14 ncv

Where God's love is, there is no fear,
because God's perfect love drives out fear.
It is punishment that makes a person fear,
so love is not made perfect in the person who fears.

1 John 4:18 ncv

You, Lord, are forgiving and good,
abounding in love to all who call to you.

Psalm 86:5 niv

Good Father, thank you for being with us day and night.
There is never a time when you are not moving on our behalf.
You don't rest. You never ignore your children. You don't ever
need a break from us, and you never turn your eyes away
from us. The love you have for our children is great. Give them
a revelation of that love. Open their eyes to see how you are
moving. May they be comforted by the fact that by day you are
directing your love, and at night your songs are with them.
May your surrounding love give them great confidence and
an unshakeable sense of security. As they learn how you are
always listening to them and always have your eyes turned
toward them, may they pursue you in the same way. May
their lives be defined by your love.

How does the love of God in your life help you to love others?

Patience

Warn those who are lazy.
Encourage those who are timid.
Take tender care of those who are weak.
Be patient with everyone.

1 Thessalonians 5:14 nlt

Be like those who through faith and patience
will receive what God has promised.

Hebrews 6:12 ncv

Be completely humble and gentle;
be patient, bearing with one another in love.

Ephesians 4:2 niv

Whoever is patient has great understanding,
but one who is quick-tempered displays folly.

Proverbs 14:29 niv

Heavenly Father, you have chosen us to parent these specific children. You know exactly what they need, and you have trusted us with their lives. We want to honor you when we parent them. May we speak gently and kindly. May our actions reflect your love and patience, and may our attitude teach them more about who you are. In each season of parenting, remind us to rely on your strength. You can do anything! When we are overwhelmed, sustain us. When we are tired and worn thin, give us new life. Help us parent in ways that draw them closer to you. We ask that your strength be made perfect in our weakness. Give us wisdom and patience where we are lacking and discernment when we don't understand what to do. We want our parenting to reflect your love.

How can you show more
patience in your life?

Peace

"I have told you these things,
so that in me you may have peace.
In this world you will have trouble.
But take heart! I have overcome the world."

John 16:33 NIV

The LORD gives his people strength.
The LORD blesses them with peace.

Psalm 29:11 NLT

May the Lord of peace himself give you peace at all times
and in every way. The Lord be with all of you.

2 Thessalonians 3:16 NIV

"I am leaving you with a gift—peace of mind and heart.
And the peace I give is a gift the world cannot give.
So don't be troubled or afraid."

John 14:27 NLT

Holy Spirit, you are welcome in our home. Come in and bring peace between these walls. Fill our hearts with love for you and for each other. Soften our harsh words and encourage us to lift each other up. If need be, make us slower to speak and slower to rise to anger. Let this home be a safe place for those who enter it. Let communication be strong and compassion abound. Strengthen the bonds between us. Let us have unity between parents and children. Build up trust as a foundation. May your presence be evident in all we say and do. Rejoice with us in our play and encourage us in our work. May those who are raised in these walls walk in peace when they leave. May they be bridge builders and peace makers, for blessed are the peace makers. Thank you for promising to be near and to give us peace.

What does peace look like for you?

Perseverance

Do you not know that in a race all the runners run,
but only one gets the prize?
Run in such a way as to get the prize.

1 Corinthians 9:24 niv

I have tried hard to find you—
don't let me wander from your commands.

Psalm 119:10 nlt

I have fought the good fight,
I have finished the race,
I have kept the faith.

2 Timothy 4:7 ncv

Let us not become weary in doing good,
for at the proper time we will reap
a harvest if we do not give up.

Galatians 6:9 niv

Father, some days are just difficult. It seems like the realization of Murphy's Law for everything. We choose to focus on you and try to make lemons out of lemonade. We push on and serve in a way that we hope pleases you. We are thankful your Spirit encourages us to keep going, but we find ourselves mentally and physically depleted at times. We have no idea how we will do it all again tomorrow. Your Word tells us to fix our eyes on you in faith. When we are weak, you are strong. We want our children to persevere regardless of any discouragement. We pray they will stand firm in their endeavors, convinced that you will honor their efforts. Give them stamina in heart and mind. When they feel like giving up, please speak words of encouragement, reminding them there is an inheritance waiting. Make it their greatest goal to please you.

What do you feel God is calling you
to persevere in right now?

Praise

Sing to the Lord a new song,
his praise from the ends of the earth,
you who go down to the sea, and all that is in it,
you islands, and all who live in them.

Isaiah 42:10 niv

Praise the Lord from the skies.
Praise him high above the earth.
Praise him, all you angels.
Praise him, all you armies of heaven.
Praise him, sun and moon.
Praise him, all you shining stars.
Praise him, highest heavens
and you waters above the sky.
Let them praise the Lord,
because they were created by his command.

Psalm 148:1-5 ncv

Heavenly Father, we are astounded by the fact that you want to reward us. You have already given us everything we could ever want or need. You deserve a multitude of accolades for the good you do in our lives, and that is why we want to sing your praise. We worship you for you are the great and holy God. There is and never will be anyone above you. May praise for you always be on our lips. Let our greatest desire be to please you in all that we say and do. Let our children grow to put you first and honor you with their dedication. May the only thing they want in return is the opportunity to cast their crowns at your feet with the greatest of thankful hearts.

What is something specific you can praise God for today?

Prayer

At each and every sunrise you will hear my voice
as I prepare my sacrifice of prayer to you.
Every morning I lay out the pieces of my life on the altar
and wait for your fire to fall upon my heart.

<small>Psalm 5:3 tpt</small>

Make your life a prayer.

<small>1 Thessalonians 5:17 tpt</small>

The Lord does not listen to the wicked,
but he hears the prayers of those who do right.

<small>Proverbs 15:29 ncv</small>

"When you pray, go away by yourself, shut the door behind you,
and pray to your Father in private. Then your Father,
who sees everything, will reward you."

<small>Matthew 6:6 nlt</small>

God, we want to hear from you. We confess that when we don't see results, or when the results are different than expected, it can be discouraging. Please, don't let this discouragement push us away from prayer. Ignite our desire to pray by helping us remember your promises. In our parenting, help us not buckle under the weight of our children's needs and give up. Hold up our arms, give them strength, and help us lift them before you once again. Take our requests and replace them with the patience to wait for your move and the confidence to know that you will. Bring to mind all the ways you have moved in their lives already. You are faithful and good.

What can you pray about right now?

Protection

My God is my rock. I can run to him for safety.
He is my shield and my saving strength,
my defender and my place of safety.
The LORD saves me from those who want to harm me.

2 SAMUEL 22:3 NCV

The LORD keeps you from all harm
and watches over your life.
The LORD keeps watch over you
as you come and go, both now and forever.

PSALM 121:7-8 NLT

Though we experience every kind of pressure, we're not
crushed. At times we don't know what to do, but quitting
is not an option. We are persecuted by others, but God has
not forsaken us. We may be knocked down, but not out.

2 CORINTHIANS 4:8-9 TPT

God our refuge, thank you for freely blessing us with peace.
Peace with you also means hostility with the world, for there is
still a battle going on. Reminded of this, we pray you will cover
our family in your armor. Whatever this day brings us, we rely
on your strength and remember the spiritual battle waging. We
sometimes forget this especially when it comes to dealing with
each other. We all have sinful natures; we face temptations
and attacks. We pray for protection over our children. May they
not give into temptation. Help them to resist by your strength. If
things get tense, help us remember to stop and pray. Thank you
for your continual protection over us.

*How hard is it for you
to lay down your battle plan
and let God be your protector?*

Purpose

Christ's resurrection is your resurrection too.
This is why we are to yearn for all that is above,
for that's where Christ sits enthroned at the place
of all power, honor, and authority.

COLOSSIANS 3:1 TPT

We know that in all things God works for the good of
those who love him, who have been called
according to his purpose.

ROMANS 8:28 NIV

My child, pay attention to my words;
listen closely to what I say.
Don't ever forget my words; keep them always in mind.

PROVERBS 4:20-21 NCV

It is God who works in you to will
and to act in order to fulfill his good purpose.

PHILIPPIANS 2:13 NIV

God who gives, we praise you for the gift of our children. Their lives bring joy to us. They are precious, and we love them. We realize that you love them even more than we do! It's an honor to be entrusted with their care. We know we are not doing this alone. We ask that you care for them too. When they have physical needs, please heal them. When their spirits are distressed because of the enemy's attacks against them, protect them and gather them under your wing. We praise you for the purpose you have given them. Bring that purpose to pass. Use them for your glory. May they dedicate their lives to serving you. Give them joy as they serve and help them discern what your will is.

How do you feel when you think about God having a special purpose for your life?

Relationships

Two are better than one,
because they have a good return for their labor:
If either of them falls down,
one can help the other up.

<small>ECCLESIASTES 4:9-10 NIV</small>

Perfume and incense bring joy to the heart,
and the pleasantness of a friend
springs from their heartfelt advice.

<small>PROVERBS 27:9 NIV</small>

Love each other with genuine affection,
and take delight in honoring each other.

<small>ROMANS 12:10 NLT</small>

God, you created us to be in relationship with others. You made us to have connection and be vulnerable with each other. Sometimes, putting ourselves out there like that can be hurtful. We pray for the people our kids will encounter. Please, give them good interactions with others. Let there be clear communication. Protect them from those who wish to harm them. Give them wisdom when they are choosing who to be close with and who to trust. When they do get hurt, help them to learn forgiveness. Don't let them build walls to keep others out; help them make bridges. Let them remain vulnerable and full of love. Most of all, let them know that you will never betray them. You will always be near to protect them.

Think of some of your closest
relationships now and
thank God for them.

Reliability

The grass dries and withers and the flowers fall off,
but the Word of the Lord endures forever!

1 Peter 1:24-25 tpt

Every good action and every perfect gift is from God. These
good gifts come down from the Creator of the sun, moon,
and stars, who does not change like their shifting shadows.

James 1:17 ncv

He will give eternal life to those who keep on doing good,
seeking after the glory and honor and immortality
that God offers.

Romans 2:7 nlt

You are near, Lord,
and all your commands are true.
Long ago I learned from your statutes
that you established them to last forever.

Psalm 119:151-152 niv

Heavenly Father, you tell us that when we cry out to you, you will answer. We believe that when we ask for your presence, you will not hold back. There is constant access to you, and we often don't take advantage of it. Strengthen our reflexes to call upon you when we are in need. May the access you've given us be a well-worn path. May our lives be marked by constant communion with you. We know that you hear us, and we know that you also hear our children. Help us to consistently point them toward you. You are their most reliable help, and we want them to lean on you through all things. Thank you for who you are. Thank you for faithfully answering us when we call.

How does it make you feel to know you can rely on God for everything?

Respect

Show respect for all people: Love the brothers and sisters
of God's family, respect God, honor the king.

1 Peter 2:17 ncv

Obey your spiritual leaders and recognize their authority,
for they keep watch over your soul without resting since
they will have to give an account to God for their work.
So it will benefit you when you make their work a
pleasure and not a heavy burden.

Hebrews 13:17 tpt

Acknowledge those who work hard among you, who care
for you in the Lord and who admonish you. Hold them in
the highest regard in love because of their work.
Live in peace with each other.

1 Thessalonians 5:12-13 niv

Perfect Father, we want to learn from you. We don't want to be the kind of parents who rule with fear. Help our parenting be worthy of our children's respect. May our relationship be mutually loving, and may we always seek to lift them up. Teach us how to have grace for them and to show mercy as you have showered grace and mercy on us. Instead of demanding that our kids follow a set of rules, help us foster an environment where honor is second nature. We want to teach them how to respect the people in authority over them but to also have respect for their peers and for themselves.

How do you show respect to the authority figures in your life?

Reward

Work willingly at whatever you do, as though you were working for the Lord rather than for people. Remember that the Lord will give you an inheritance as your reward, and that the Master you are serving is Christ.

COLOSSIANS 3:23-24 NLT

"Love your enemies, do good to them, and lend to them without expecting to get anything back. Then your reward will be great, and you will be children of the Most High, because he is kind to the ungrateful and wicked."

LUKE 6:35 NIV

Without faith living within us it would be impossible to please God. For we come to God in faith knowing that he is real and that he rewards the faith of those who passionately seek him.

HEBREWS 11:6 TPT

Lord, teach us to be mindful of these days and of the culture in our home. Give us wisdom and insight to see the culture we have and what could change to bring you more glory. We want our children to know that they can do hard things. Just because something is difficult doesn't mean it isn't worth doing. We want them to grow in perseverance and endurance, two necessities for a good life. Teach us how to teach them. Let us model by example. Please, show them the rewards of hard work. It is by your immeasurable strength that we can do hard things. In our weakness, you make us strong. Thank you. Give us the endurance needed to do the hard task of parenting. May we also see the rewards of the hard labor and be encouraged by them.

How does it make you feel knowing that God will reward you for your diligence?

Salvation

"This is how God loved the world: He gave his one and
only Son, so that everyone who believes in him
will not perish but have eternal life."

JOHN 3:16 NLT

The wages of sin is death, but the gift of God
is eternal life in Christ Jesus our Lord.

ROMANS 6:23 NIV

By grace you have been saved by faith. Nothing you did
could ever earn this salvation, for it was the love gift
from God that brought us to Christ!

EPHESIANS 2:8 TPT

If you openly declare that Jesus is Lord and believe in your
heart that God raised him from the dead, you will be saved.

ROMANS 10:9 NLT

We thank you for your mighty power, God. You are mighty to save, and we praise you for saving us out of darkness and bringing us into glorious life. You have given us a purpose: to bring you glory and to preach your gospel. You have specifically given us these children to disciple. Show us the depth of purpose in the task in front of us. As we lean into that purpose, remind us that it is not our job to bring our kids to salvation; it's our job to teach them the gospel. You are the only one mighty enough to save. Holy Spirit, work in their hearts. May their hearts be fertile ground for you. Keep them close to you and pursue them to the end just like you promised.

How do you respond to the message of salvation?

Serving

Each of you should use whatever gift you have received to serve others, as faithful stewards of God's grace in its various forms. If anyone serves, they should do so with the strength God provides, so that in all things God may be praised through Jesus Christ.

1 Peter 4:10-11 niv

Always give yourselves fully to the work of the Lord, because you know that your labor in the Lord is not in vain.

1 Corinthians 15:58 niv

You were called to freedom…
do not use your freedom as an opportunity for the flesh, but through love serve one another.

Galatians 5:13 esv

Heavenly Father, thank you for the abundant ways you have gifted our children. Thank you for the spiritual gifts you have given them. Help us foster those gifts with love and kindness. Soften our hearts toward them. Open our eyes to see them how you created them. You have given us the privilege of being their teacher, encourager, and caregiver. We don't want to take those roles for granted. As they step out in their gifts, may we be quick to speak life-giving words. When they stumble, may we be a comfort to them and an example of how your love is not contingent on how well we do. May we continuously point them to the cross instead of toward shallow spiritual goals. We know that you have wonderful plans for each of them. Help us to encourage them as they walk the paths that you have made for them specifically.

Is there a way you can serve God and your children today?

Strength

God is our refuge and strength,
an ever-present help in trouble.

Psalm 46:1-3 niv

The Lord is faithful, and he will strengthen you
and protect you from the evil one.

2 Thessalonians 3:3 niv

"Don't be afraid, for I am with you.
Don't be discouraged, for I am your God.
I will strengthen you and help you.
I will hold you up with my victorious right hand."

Isaiah 41:10 nlt

Lord, don't be far away.
You are my strength; hurry to help me.

Psalm 22:19 ncv

Jesus, King of the upside-down kingdom, we praise you because your ways are higher than ours. The way you operate is always holy and good. Thank you for doing the heavy lifting for us. We rely on your strength and power. Especially in our parenting, we often feel weak. We don't always know what to do or how to help our kids. But in this weakness of parenting, your power is seen most vividly. When we feel inadequate, will you show yourself sufficient? When we are unable to lift these burdens, will you strong man them off our backs? When we are at a loss, will you help us find our way? Keep us from the temptation to operate in our own power. When these moments come, gently remind us that your power rests on us when we are weak, not when we are trying to be the strong ones. Thank you for working your power in our home.

What makes you feel strong?

Stress

As pressure and stress bear down on me,
I find joy in your commands.
Psalm 119:143 NLT

Praise the Lord, my soul;
all my inmost being, praise his holy name.
Praise the Lord, my soul,
and forget not all his benefits—
who forgives all your sins
and heals all your diseases,
who redeems your life from the pit
and crowns you with love and compassion,
who satisfies your desires with good things
so that your youth is renewed like the eagle's.
Psalm 103:1-5 NIV

Heavenly Father, help us to find our rest in you. No matter how busy life gets, help us to trust in you for strength. As we pour our lives out for our children, help us to seek your renewal. Refresh our spirits when we are overwhelmed. Help us teach our children how to stay rooted in your love rather than striving to complete a to-do list. Give them true rest and draw them closer to you. Teach them to quietly trust you when they are stressed out. When they are overburdened, give them the grace to surrender their troubles to you. May they rely on your strength rather than give in to anxiety. Teach them to lay down their cares at your feet because you care for them.

When was the last time you were able to let go of stress and just sit with God?

Teaching

All Scripture is inspired by God and is profitable for
teaching, for rebuking, for correcting, for training in
righteousness, so that the man of God may be complete,
equipped in every good work.

2 Timothy 3:16-17 csb

Let each generation tell its children of your mighty acts;
let them proclaim your power.

Psalm 145:4 nlt

"Go therefore and make disciples of all the nations,
baptizing them in the name of the Father and of the Son
and of the Holy Spirit, teaching them to observe
all things that I have commanded you."

Matthew 28:19-20 nkjv

Jesus, you spent much of your time on earth teaching. Most will acknowledge you as a great teacher even if they do not accept you as Lord. How can one acknowledge your great teaching and not accept what you say as truth? May our kids be students in your house. May they learn from you, follow your instructions, and find you to be Lord of their lives and not just a teacher. May they sit at your feet and soak in all you have to say. When they need guidance, may they turn to your Word and to prayer. Let your Word come alive to them and bring them great joy. Through your Word, bring them peace. Lead them on the paths that are straight. Make us all humble learners of your perfect will.

When is it most difficult to teach your children about the Lord?

Thankfulness

I have not stopped giving thanks for you,
remembering you in my prayers.

EPHESIANS 1:16 NIV

Giving thanks is a sacrifice that truly honors me.
If you keep to my path,
I will reveal to you the salvation of God.

PSALM 50:23 NLT

Rejoice always, pray continually, give thanks in all
circumstances; for this is God's will for you in Christ Jesus.

1 THESSALONIANS 5:16–18 NIV

You can pass through his open gates
with the password of praise.
Come right into his presence with thanksgiving.
Come bring your thank offering to him
and affectionately bless his beautiful name!

PSALM 100:4 TPT

God, we give you thanks. Your abounding goodness toward our family is enough to leave us singing your praises for the rest of our lives. Cultivate thankful hearts in our kids. Our natural pride wants to rise up and push back against gratitude, but we know the powerful work that comes from giving thanks. Change our lives and perspectives through thankfulness. Let hearts of gratitude grow within us. As the kids grow, may thanksgiving flourish in their lives and choke out weeds of bitterness, grumbling, complaining, and discontentment. May they notice big things to give thanks for, and may they search for the little things. May all this thankfulness pile up as stones on an altar, big and small, to give glory to you.

What can you thank God for right now?

Trust

Those who know the LORD trust him,
because he will not leave those who come to him.

PSALM 9:10 NCV

I trust in you, LORD. I say, "You are my God."
My whole life is in your hands.
Save me from the hands of my enemies.
Save me from those who are chasing me.

PSALM 31:14-15 NIV

Yes, the LORD is for me; he will help me.
I will look in triumph at those who hate me.
It is better to take refuge in the LORD
than to trust in people.

PSALM 118:7-8 NLT

God, you have proven yourself to be trustworthy. We praise you for being a safe place. You have created us to be in relationship with you and with others; relationships with others are often precarious. We are all sinful and thus prone to hurt each other and betray trust. You, however, are perfect and good; you will never betray us. Help our children to find you as a safe refuge as well. May they cast their hopes and trust in you, looking to you to be their safe place even more than they look to us. We will fail them at some point. Let even our failure be an opportunity for them to turn to you: the one who will never betray or fail them.

How do you know
that God is trustworthy?

Truth

"When he, the Spirit of truth, comes,
he will guide you into all the truth."

JOHN 16:13 NIV

The very essence of your words is truth;
all your just regulations will stand forever.

PSALM 119:160 NLT

"If you abide in My word, you are My disciples indeed.
And you shall know the truth,
and the truth shall make you free."

JOHN 8:31-32 NKJV

Teach me your way, O LORD,
that I may walk in your truth;
unite my heart to fear your name.

PSALM 86:11 ESV

Jesus, you are the way, the truth, and the life. No one comes to the Father except through you. You are the true Son of God. We confess all these things and hold them as truth in our lives. We ask that our children know you for who you are. May they not be deceived by the world. Perhaps others want you to be more accepting of sin and the lifestyles that sinful people want to live. Help our children see your holiness in opposition to this lie. Maybe the lie is that you are not the only way and there are many ways. Help our kids hold fast to you as the one true Son of God. Let our children not take offense at you or at your Word but embrace it as the truth by which they live.

What steps can you take to be more
truthful in your everyday life?

Understanding

Wisdom is a deep well of understanding
Opened up within you as a fountain of life for others.

PROVERBS 16:22 TPT

The teaching of your word gives light,
so even the simple can understand.

PSALM 119:130 NLT

Give me understanding,
so that I may keep your law and obey it with all my heart.

PSALM 119:34 NIV

Don't act thoughtlessly, but understand what the Lord
wants you to do.

EPHESIANS 5:17 NLT

Holy Spirit, thank you for bringing an understanding we could not gain elsewhere. You make known to us the mysteries of God. It is by your teaching that we know his wonderful grace. Your very presence is a gift. Be with our children. Let them be filled by you and know your power is not limited by their age or size. You want them to know you, and you want to move in their lives as you do in ours. Help them not to shrink away from the things you want them to do and say. May they boldly follow your lead. Let them be children who are full of courage, speaking the wisdom and truth you give them. Give them greater understanding of your will and way as they seek you with all their hearts.

How do you seek to understand
God's will each day?

Victory

The horse is made ready for the day of battle,
But the victory rests with the LORD.

PROVERBS 21:31 NIV

Every child of God defeats this evil world,
and we achieve this victory through our faith.

1 JOHN 5:4 NLT

Say to the anxious and fearful,
"Be strong and never afraid.
Look, here comes your God!
He is breaking through to give you victory!
He comes to avenge your enemies.
With divine retribution he comes to save you!"

ISAIAH 35:4 TPT

Jesus, you are the resurrection. What a glorious truth! The veil has been torn, and now we have complete access to God through you. You conquered sin and death. Victory is not something we will one day grasp; you present it to us right now. Death has no power over us anymore, and we are free in you. We will join the victory march because we share your triumph. Thank you for granting us eternal life with you. Let this truth free us of the fear of death. When fear grips us about those we love, especially our kids, remind us of your resurrection. We pray that our kids will believe in you and live eternally with us in heaven. We trust in your sovereign control over their lives and thank you for the freedom you have given us.

You win with Jesus in your life! Can you think of the last victory you experienced?

Wisdom

Wisdom will come into your mind,
and knowledge will be pleasing to you.
Good sense will protect you;
understanding will guard you
It will keep you from the wicked,
from those whose words are bad.

PROVERBS 2:10-12 NCV

Wisdom and money can get you almost anything,
but only wisdom can save your life.

ECCLESIASTES 7:12 NLT

If any of you lacks wisdom, you should ask God,
who gives generously to all without finding fault,
and it will be given to you.

JAMES 1:5 NIV

Thank you, God, for your Word. It is full of wisdom and truth. It enables us to discern between worldly wisdom which leads to death and your wisdom which leads to life. We ask that our children be life-long learners of your wisdom. May they learn to love your Word and esteem it highly. Teach them discernment so they will know the difference between worldly and godly wisdom. May they be fair and honest. We pray they will be people who help other people. May they not look down on the troubled, but may they point others to you and do good to them. Teach them what true goodness is. Thank you for the people our children are becoming. Already, you are guiding them in wisdom.

How can you use God's wisdom to make better choices?

Worry

Leave all your cares and anxieties at the feet of the Lord,
and measureless grace will strengthen you.

Psalm 55:22 tpt

"Who of you by worrying
can add a single hour to your life?"

Luke 12:25 niv

Worry weighs a person down;
an encouraging word cheers a person up.

Proverbs 12:25 nlt

Do not worry about anything, but pray and ask God for
everything you need, always giving thanks. And God's
peace, which is so great we cannot understand it,
will keep your hearts and minds in Christ Jesus.

Philippians 4:6-7 ncv

God, we surrender our worries to you. Sometimes, all the things we have to remember are overwhelming. All the responsibility can drown us in worries and cares. We open our hands and offer those cares up to you right now. Thank you for the deep compassion and empathy you have for even the small, mundane things that stress us out. Quiet our minds. Help us do what we need to do while letting go of things that don't matter. We confess our worries to you and ask you to bring us peace. If our children are worried or anxious over anything, we pray they will learn to surrender their cares to you. Together, let us consider the flowers and the birds that you take care of and rest in the promise that you will care for us too.

What worries can you
hand over to God today?

BroadStreet Publishing Group, LLC.
Savage, Minnesota, USA
Broadstreetpublishing.com

PRAYERS & PROMISES FOR *Parents*

© 2023 by BroadStreet Publishing®

978-1-4245-6666-2
978-1-4245-6527-6 (eBook)

Design and typesetting by Garborg Design Works | garborgdesign.com
Compiled and edited by Michelle Winger | literallyprecise.com

Printed in China.

23   24   25   26   27   28   29   7   6   5   4   3   2   1